TIMELINES IN SCIENCE

SCIENCE OF THE ATOMIC AGE

Craig Boutland

ROSEN PUBLISHING

Published in 2025 by The Rosen Publishing Group, Inc.
2544 Clinton Street, Buffalo, NY 14224

Portions of this work were originally authored by Charlie Samuels and published as *The Age of the Atom*. All new material in this edition was authored by Craig Boutland.

PICTURE CREDITS
t=top, b=bottom, l=left, r=right, c=center

Front Cover: iStock: zambeziShark tl; Shutterstock: F Bastijanic tr, Evanovestro main, K Nalok tc.
Inside: Alamy: CBW 26, GL Archive 53t, The Picture Art Collection 23; Library of Congress: 17, 21, 25, 27, 33; NOAA: 56; Public Domain: 8, 60, Paul Ehrenfest 24, Ji-Elle 57, National Library of Austria/Adam Cuerdon 22, Nobel Foundation/Erik Lindberg/Jonathunder 9, Richard Varcoe on behalf of Caladan Oceanic 61, Thinkstock/Photos.com 13t&b, 14, 16, 19, 29; Robert Hunt Library: 43, 48, 49, 50t&b; Science Photo Library: Dr Jeremy Burgess 40, CERN 32, David Parker & Julian Baum 34; Shutterstock: Mark Agnor 7, Eniko Balogh 51, Timo Fleeff 6, Adam Gryko 31, Steffen Hoejager 47, Shi Luba 28, I Pilon 5, Dario Sabijak 10, Ben Schonewille 59, Alex Stokes 44, Bruno Vittorio 11, Brad Whitsitt 18; Topfoto: 41, 45, IMAGNO/Austrian Archives 53b, Photri 55, Pictures from History 58, The Granger Collection 42, Topham Picturepoint 36, 37, ullsteinbild 52.

All other artwork and illustrations Brown Bear Books Ltd

Cataloging-in-Publication Data

Names: Boutland, Craig.
Title: The atomic age / Craig Boutland.
Description: Buffalo, NY : Rosen Young Adult, 2025. | Series: Timelines in science | Includes glossary and index.
Identifiers: ISBN 9781499477795 (pbk.) | ISBN 9781499477801 (library bound) | ISBN 9781499477818 (ebook)
Subjects: LCSH: Inventions–History–20th century–Juvenile literature. | Discoveries in science–History–20th century–Juvenile literature. | Nuclear warfare–History–Juvenile literature.
Classification: LCC Q180.55.D57 B68 202 | DDC 509–dc23

Manufactured in the United States of America

CPSIA Compliance Information: Batch #CSRYA25.
For further information, contact Rosen Publishing at 1-800-237-9932.

CONTENTS

Introduction

The first half of the 20th century was dominated by two world wars. As always, conflict encouraged technological development as combatants raced to gain the upper hand.

The most promising area of scientific exploration was the nature of atoms, the particles that made them up, and the power they contained. Nowhere did increased knowledge of the atomic and subatomic world have more profound effects than in electronics. The work of theoretical physicists such as Albert Einstein, who sought to understand the very nature of the universe itself, led to a practical appreciation of radio waves and the development of radio and TV. In transportation, meanwhile, the coming of the airplane and the automobile were to be equally revolutionary. Not for the first time in history, scientific advances were changing the ways people communicated—and even how they thought.

The Influence of Warfare

In the shadow of the two world wars (1914–1918 and 1939–1945), weaponry became more powerful; an understanding of radio waves led to the technology of radar. Medical care advanced, too, with the creation of the first antibiotic, penicillin. In the early 1940s, scientists in Britain and the United States experimented with unlocking the power of the atom. Just three years after they created the first controlled nuclear chain reaction in a room in Chicago, atom bombs were dropped on Japan.

About This Book

This book uses timelines to describe scientific and technological advances from about 1900 to about 1950. A continuous timeline of the period runs along the bottom of all the pages. Its entries are color-coded to indicate the different fields of science to which they belong. Each chapter also has its own subject-specific timeline, which runs vertically down the edge of the page.

Radio spread rapidly through the 1920s and 1930s as a means of mass communication. It gave people increased access to everything from sports to politics.

Nobel and High Explosive

Alfred Nobel invented explosives that were more powerful than anything seen before. He also created the Nobel Prizes, which are awarded for outstanding achievement, especially in science.

Alfred Bernhard Nobel (1833–1896) was a prolific Swedish inventor. His father, Immanuel, was an engineer and an inventor. When his business failed in Sweden, he moved to St. Petersburg, Russia. There, Immanuel opened a mechanical workshop that made equipment for the Russian army. In 1842, Alfred and his mother joined Immanuel in St. Petersburg. Alfred was educated by private tutors. By the age of 17, he could speak five languages and showed great ability in the sciences, particularly chemistry. He was sent to Europe to continue his studies and in 1850, met Ascanio Sobrero in Paris. Sobrero was an Italian chemist. He

A photograph of Alfred Nobel, taken by the Swedish photographer Gösta Florman (1831-1900).

TIMELINE

1900–1901

KEY:

Biology and Medicine

Engineering and Invention

Chemistry and Physics

1900 Cuban-born U.S. physiologist Aristides Agramonte y Simoni discovers that yellow fever is transmitted through the bite of a mosquito.

1900

1900 Austrian neurologist Sigmund Freud publishes his influential book *The Interpretation of Dreams.*

1900 The rigid airship LZ-1, designed by German engineer Graf Ferdinand von Zeppelin, makes its first flight.

had recently invented a powerful explosive—nitroglycerin. This was a combination of glycerol and nitric acid. The problem was that nitroglycerin was unstable, and therefore extremely dangerous. Nobel became fascinated by the question of how to make nitroglycerin safe to use. He realized the commercial potential if he succeeded. Using family money, he invested in a factory in Sweden where he hoped to

Timeline

1857 Nobel awarded his first patent, for a gas meter

1864 Factory in Sweden explodes, killing Nobel's brother and other workers

1867 Awarded a patent for dynamite

1875 Awarded a patent for gelignite

1895 Makes his will leaving almost all his wealth to funding five Nobel Prizes

Gelignite and dynamite are used in the mining and demolition industries.

1900 German physicist Max Planck proposes the quantum theory: that radiation is emitted in separate "packets," or quanta.

1901 Japanese-born U.S. chemist Jokichi Takamine isolates epinephrine (adrenaline).

1901 German physicist Karl Ferdinand Braun invents the crystal detector for tuning a radio.

1900

1901

1900 U.S. inventor Thomas Edison invents the nickel-iron accumulator (known as the Ni-Fe cell).

1901 Italian physicist Guglielmo Marconi makes the first transatlantic radio transmission.

As a young man, Nobel became fascinated with the potential of nitroglycerin.

manufacture a safe substance. However, the dangers of nitroglycerin were shown all too clearly when, in 1864, an explosion at the factory killed his brother Emil.

Gelignite

Undeterred, Alfred built a factory in a more remote location. His research paid off when he added an inert, absorbent substance called diatomaceous earth to nitroglycerin and found that this stabilized the explosive. His patent for the new explosive, dynamite, was granted in 1867.

Nobel went on to create two more important explosives. In 1875, he patented gelignite, which was even more stable and powerful than dynamite and, crucially, came as a soft, malleable substance that could be pushed into predrilled holes or wrapped around rocks. Then, in 1887, he invented ballistite. This was a

TIMELINE
1902–1903

KEY:
- Biology and Medicine
- Engineering and Invention
- Astronomy and Math

1902 French meteorologist Léon Teisserenc de Bort distinguishes the stratosphere and troposphere layers in Earth's atmosphere.

1902

1902 French surgeon Alexis Carrel develops a technique for joining blood vessels end to end with fine stitches (sutures).

1902 German chemist Emil Fischer determines that proteins are polypeptides, made up from chains of amino acids.

propellant for artillery shells. It was smokeless and an advance on the smoky gunpowder previously used.

These inventions made Nobel enormously wealthy. He invested his money in armaments companies that increased his wealth. He was criticized, however, as being a dealer in death, and this criticism seems to have affected Nobel deeply. He had no children, and in 1895, he wrote a will leaving the bulk of his wealth to fund five prizes. These were to be administered by the Swedish Academy of Sciences, of which Nobel had become a member in 1884. Three prizes were in science, for Physics, Chemistry, and Medicine or Physiology. One was for literary excellence and another for contributions to human fraternity, commonly called the Peace Prize. A sixth prize, for Economics, was added in 1968.

The medal for the Nobel Prize in Physiology that was awarded to Mayo Clinic researchers in 1950.

1903 U.S. brothers Orville and Wilbur Wright make the first sustained flight in a heavier-than-air airplane.

1903 German surgeon Georg Perthes first uses X-rays to treat cancerous tumors.

1903 Russian astrophysicist Konstantin Tsiolkovsky proposes the first practical theory of rocket propulsion.

1903

1903 Dutch physiologist Willem Einthoven invents the electrocardiograph for recording electrical activity in the heart.

1903 Russian physiologist Ivan Pavlov develops the concept of the conditioned reflex (the way in which an action can be influenced by previous repetitive behavior).

The Invention of Radio

Radio uses electromagnetic radiation, known as radio waves, which travel at the speed of light. It was called "wireless" to distinguish it from telegraphs and telephones.

Radios became commonplace in many homes in the United States and Europe during the 1920s.

TIMELINE
1904–1905

KEY:
- Biology and Medicine
- Engineering and Invention
- Astronomy and Math
- Chemistry and Physics

1904 English physicist J. J. Thompson puts forward his model of the atom: a spherical mass of positively charged matter with electrons embedded in it.

1904

1904 The first section of the New York City subway opens, with electric trains serving 28 stations.

1904 English engineer John Fleming invents the diode valve (vacuum tube).

Radio dates from the late–19th century. The Scottish physicist James Clerk Maxwell predicted mathematically the existence of electromagnetic radiation in 1864. He decided that light is just one part of the spectrum of electromagnetic radiation. In 1887, German physicist Heinrich Hertz discovered a new type of radiation: radio waves.

Radio Waves

In 1890, French physicist Édouard Branly devised the first method of detecting radio waves using a "coherer," a sealed glass tube containing iron filings and an electrode at each end. When radio waves are present, the filings stick together and conduct electricity to form part of a circuit. English physicist Oliver Lodge improved the coherer in 1894 and used it together with a spark transmitter to send Morse code messages a distance of 490 feet (150 m). Russian physicist Aleksandr Popov conducted similar experiments a year later.

Unaware of these developments, Italian physicist Guglielmo Marconi also began experimenting with radio in 1894. He invented a radio antenna and the use of a ground (earth) with the apparatus. He could soon transmit coded messages more than 1.8 miles (3 km). The

Timeline

1864 Radio waves predicted

1887 Discovery of radio waves

1890 Coherer for detecting radio waves

1894 Marconi's first radio transmissions

1903 Amplitude modulation (AM)

1904 Diode vacuum tube

1906 Triode vacuum tube

1933 Frequency modulation (FM)

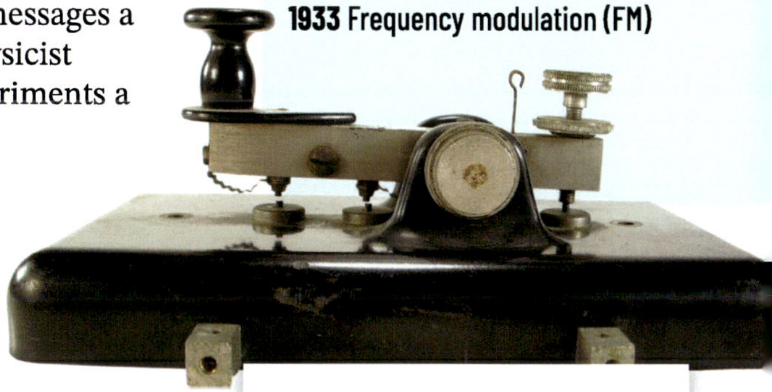

Some of the earliest transmissions used Morse code signals.

1904 German astrophysicist Johannes Hartmann reveals the presence of interstellar matter in space.

1904 English chemist Arthur Harden discovers coenzymes, molecules that are needed to trigger the action of enzymes.

1905 French physicist Paul Langevin applies the electron theory to magnetic phenomena.

1905 German-born U.S. physicist Albert Einstein publishes his special theory of relativity, one of the most important theories in science.

1905 French psychologists devise a method of testing intelligence and ascribing an intelligence quotient (IQ).

1905 U.S. engineer Almon Strowger perfects the dial switch telephone.

1904

1905

Amplitude Modulation

Radiotelephony relies on modulation: altering a constant signal by a varying one. An audio-frequency signal from a microphone is amplified to vary an oscillator's radio-frequency signal, which is reamplified then transmitted. At the receiver, an antenna picks up the transmitted signal. It is amplified before being demodulated and amplified to reproduce the original audio signal in a loudspeaker.

invention, known as radiotelegraphy, developed rapidly, especially after Marconi moved to England in 1896. By 1901, he could transmit signals in Morse code across the Atlantic Ocean.

So far, radio was an improvement on the telegraph because it did not need wires to transmit signals. But could radio be made to carry human voices, like the telephone? This question led to the development of radiotelephony, when the Canadian-born U.S. electrical engineer Reginald Fessenden invented modulation. Radiotelegraphy sends out pulses of short and long signals (the dots and dashes of Morse code). In radiotelephony,

The strength or the frequency of the constant carrier wave can be modulated.

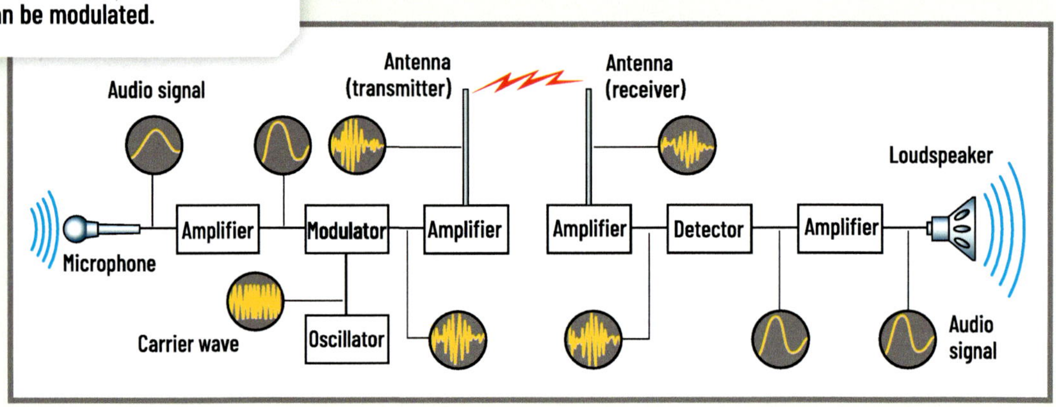

TIMELINE
1906–1907

KEY:
Biology and Medicine
Astronomy and Math
Chemistry and Physics

1906 French mathematician Maurice Fréchet introduces functional calculus.

1906 New-Zealand born physicist Ernest Rutherford deduces that alpha particles (produced by radium emission) are helium nuclei.

1906

1906 English geologist Richard Oldham deduces that Earth's core is molten.

1906 Austrian physician Clemens von Pirquet shows that hay fever is an allergic reaction to pollen and devises the term "allergy."

the transmitter sends out a continuous signal, a carrier wave, whose amplitude (strength) is varied (modulated) in step with the variations in the sound signals from a microphone. It allows the transmission of a range of sounds. Fessenden demonstrated amplitude modulation (AM) in 1903. By 1906, speech and music were transmitted from a radio station in Massachusetts.

Marconi built a radio station in Ireland to transmit signals across the Atlantic.

Improved Detectors

The new system needed a better detector. It came in the form of an improved crystal detector. The detector connected to the radio circuit by an adjustable thin wire, which earned it the nickname "cat's whisker." In 1917, Marconi began making VHF (very high frequency) transmissions. By 1924, Marconi was also sending speech signals from England to Australia using shortwave radio.

Radio receivers improved in 1912, when Fessenden devised the heterodyne circuit, which allowed more selective tuning. In 1933, American engineer Edwin Armstrong invented FM (frequency modulation). In this technique, the frequency (not the amplitude) of the transmitted carrier wave is modulated by the broadcast signal. As a result, transmission was less sensitive to static, producing an increase in the quality of the received sound.

Marconi developed radio into a reliable means of international communications.

1907 Belgian-born U.S. chemist Leo Baekeland invents Bakelite plastic.

1907 Swiss chemist Jacques Brandenburger prepares cellophane.

1907

1907 U.S. zoologist Ross Harrison begins the technique of in vitro tissue culture (growing tissues in glass laboratory apparatus).

1907 German chemist Emil Fischer confirms that proteins are made up of chains of amino acids by synthesizing a polypeptide.

The First Automobiles

The automobile was the end result of a long effort to invent a motorized road vehicle. Early machines used a steam engine, the only motive power then available.

A father and son show off their Model T Ford in the United States in the 1920s.

TIMELINE

1908–1909

KEY:

- Biology and Medicine
- Engineering and Invention
- Astronomy and Math
- Chemistry and Physics

1908 Danish astronomer Ejnar Hertzsprung introduces a method of classifying stars by plotting a graph of luminosity against temperature.

1908 The Tunguska event occurs in Siberia; it may have been a comet colliding with Earth.

1908

1908 U.S. physicist William Coolidge uses tungsten to make an incandescent filament lamp.

1908 French anthropologist Marcellin Boule reconstructs the first complete Neanderthal skeleton.

In 1770, French engineer Nicolas-Joseph Cugnot built a three-wheel gun carriage, powered by a two-cylinder steam engine. Traveling at 3 miles (5 km) per hour, it had the world's first motor accident when it demolished a wall. German engineer Charles Dietz built another three-wheel machine in 1835. It used a pair of rocking cylinders that moved a chain drive to the rear wheels.

The first Benz car 1885

Panhard and Levassor 1894

Daimler 1886

Model T Ford 1908

Timeline

1770 Cugnot's second steam-powered gun carriage

1829 Steam-powered road vehicle

1865 Lightweight steam carriage

1885 Benz three-wheeler

1886 Daimler four-wheel car

1893 Benz four-wheel car

1896 First U.S. automobile (Duryea) on sale

1908 Model T Ford

The first cars had only three wheels, but engineers soon favored the stability of four wheels. By the time of the Model T, tiller steering had been replaced by a steering wheel.

1908 U.S. inventor Elmer Sperry produces a gyroscope for ships.

1909 English physiologist Henry Dale discovers oxytocin, the hormone that controls the womb during childbirth.

1909 French aviator Louis Blériot flies across the English Channel.

1908

1909

1908 The first Ford Model T rolls off the assembly line in Detroit, Michigan.

1909 Danish chemist Søren Sørensen introduces the concept of pH, which measures hydrogen ion concentration to show the strength of an acid or alkali.

By 1894, speed and endurance races were held in France.

Experiments with steam vehicles continued to produce tractors or multipassenger carriages rather than personal vehicles. In England, William Murdock ran a model steam-powered road vehicle in 1784, and in 1789 U.S. inventor Oliver Evans fitted a high-pressure engine to a four-wheel vehicle. Back in England, Richard Trevithick built a vehicle in 1801 with large driving wheels. It reached a speed of 10 miles (16 km) per hour. In 1829, English inventor Goldsworthy Gurney began a steam coach service, with vehicles averaging a speed of 15 miles (24 km) per hour. Around 1865, New Yorker Richard Dudgeon built a lightweight steam carriage, and in 1878 French engineer Amédée Bollée's carriage *La Mancelle* had a front-mounted engine driving the rear wheels and a speed of up to 25 miles (40 km) per hour. However, just as they were improving, steam carriages designed for road travel declined in the face of competition from the railroads.

The Gasoline Engine

The next development came from Germans Karl Benz and Gottlieb Daimler. They saw the potential of the gasoline engine. Benz's first three-wheel car dates from 1885. Its 1-horsepower engine reached

TIMELINE
1909–1910

KEY:

Biology and Medicine

Engineering and Invention

Chemistry and Physics

1909 "SOS" is introduced as the international radio distress signal.

1909 Russian-born U.S. chemist Phoebus Levene identifies the sugar ribose in some nucleic acids (now known as RNA, ribonucleic acid).

1909

1909 Danish botanist Wilhelm Johannsen coins the term "gene" for the factor that carries inheritable characteristics.

8 miles (13 km) per hour. Daimler built his first car in 1886, with a gasoline engine in a heavier four-wheel vehicle.

By 1891, French engineers René Panhard and Émile Levassor had front-mounted Daimler engines to drive rear wheels. The cars had modern steering, a gear box, and a friction clutch. By 1893, Benz was making the more stable four-wheel cars with 3-horsepower engines. The same year, U.S. inventors Charles and Frank Duryea built the first gasoline-engine car. The first U.S.-made auto (Duryea) went on sale in 1896.

Industrialist Henry Ford revolutionized carmaking by introducing mass-production techniques at the start of the 20th century. As a chassis moved along an assembly line, workers added parts. In 1908, the method produced the Model T, or "Tin Lizzy," as it was known. "You can have it in any color as long as it's black," declared Ford. The motor age was born.

Ford's Assembly Line

Henry Ford's vision was to make the car available to all Americans by reducing the cost. He introduced a system in which the car chassis moved slowly along while workers repeated the same task on every chassis. A car could now be made in 1 hour 33 minutes, rather than the 12 hours it had taken before. Ford paid his workers better than average wages to keep his workforce stable. By 1914, one of Ford's own workers could buy a Model T with four months' pay.

The Model T had high axles to cope with rough, unsurfaced rural roads and tracks.

1910 New-Zealand born English physicist Ernest Rutherford proves the existence of the atom.

1910 French engineer Henri Fabre builds the first seaplane.

1910

1910 U.S. pathologist Francis Peyton Rous identifies the first virus that causes cancer.

1910 U.S. airman Eugene Fly makes the first airplane flight off the deck of a ship.

The Airplane

Even before the invention of flying machines, people wanted to imitate birds and take to the air. It was not until the 20th century that the ambition was fully realized.

The Wright Brothers' *Flyer* was a glider with an engine attached for power.

TIMELINE
1911-1912

KEY:

Biology and Medicine

Engineering and Invention

Chemistry and Physics

1911 Dutch physicist Heike Kamerlingh Onnes discovers superconductivity, the total loss of electrical resistance that some substances have at very low temperatures.

1911

1911 German physicist Karl Ferdinand Braun devises a scanning system for cathode-ray tubes, later used for TV and radar.

1911 English physiologist Henry Dale identifies histamine, a substance released by the body to fight allergies.

The first heavier-than-air machines to fly were kites, invented by the Chinese around 1000 BCE. By the late-19th century, human-carrying kites were built. English soldier Baden Baden-Powell designed one in 1894, and American showman "Colonel" Samuel Cody improved it in 1901. But real progress did not come until people began to experiment with gliders.

Timeline

1808 Unmanned glider

1848 Steam-powered model airplane

1853 Human-carrying glider

1890 Unmanned steam-powered airplane

1891 Steerable human-carrying glider

1903 First sustained flight in gasoline-engined airplane

Off the Ground

The first person to build a steerable glider that could be controlled in flight was German Otto Lilienthal. His first flight was made in 1891. His early machines copied birds' wings, but later he added a tail for stability and came up with the idea of two pairs of wings. This arrangement, later called a biplane, remained a feature of nearly all early flying machines. In the United States, Wilbur Wright and his brother Orville read about Lilienthal's pioneering work, which would influence their

Otto Lilienthal makes his first glider flight in 1891. He later died in a glider crash.

1912 The largest lizard, the Komodo dragon, is discovered in Indonesia.

1912 Grand Central Station in New York, the largest railroad station in the world, is completed.

1912

1912 German chemist Paul Ehrlich introduces acriflavine for use as an antiseptic.

1912 The SS *Titanic* sinks on its first voyage, with the loss of more than 1,500 lives.

The Wright *Flyer*

The Wright brothers' *Flyer* used a light aluminum gasoline engine to power two "pusher" propellers. The propellers rotated in opposite directions to keep torque from rotating the whole airplane. The pilot steered using a combination of the rudder and "wing warping." This involved flexing the ends of the wings (like a bird) to bank the plane into a turn. The pilot used the elevator to make it climb and descend. After several flights, with the brothers taking turns as pilot, the plane was damaged. It never flew again.

experiments. By 1903, they had perfected their human-carrying gliders.

Powered Flight

By the early 20th century, engineers had an "airframe." Now all they needed was a suitable power source. At the time, the steam engine was the only possibility. Various inventors tried their hands at flying steam-powered mono- and biplanes, but none succeeded in flying more than short distances before crashing. Steam engines were just too heavy for the task. The alternative was the gasoline engine. In 1903, Samuel Langley built a full-sized airplane with a gasoline engine. Two attempts failed—the machine

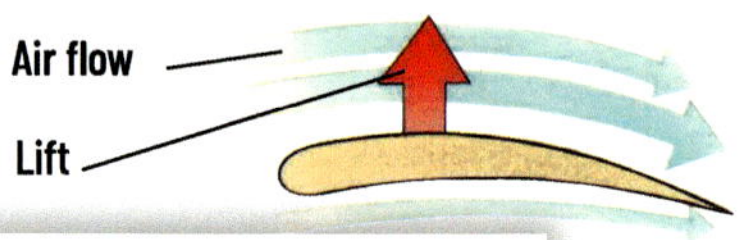

The *Flyer's* wings produced lift because of their shape. Air flowing over the top of the wing has farther to travel and moves faster than the air below. The faster air moves, the lower its pressure. This causes low pressure above the wing and high pressure below it, producing lift.

TIMELINE
1913–1914

KEY:

- Biology and Medicine
- Engineering and Invention
- Astronomy and Math
- Chemistry and Physics

1913 U.S. physicist William Coolidge invents the X-ray tube.

1913 U.S. chemist William Burton patents a method for "cracking" crude oil by breaking it down into simpler compounds using heat.

1913

1913 French physicist Charles Fabry reveals the existence of the ozone layer in Earth's upper atmosphere.

French aviator Louis Blériot's airplane lies on the ground near Dover, United Kingdom, after his flight from France in 1909—the first long flight over a body of water.

crashed into Washington, D.C.'s, Potomac River. The Wright brothers built their own gasoline engine out of lightweight aluminum and attached it to one of their gliders. The launch of this machine at Kitty Hawk, North Carolina, on December 17, 1903 heralded the start of sustained heavier-than-air flight. For the first time, a human flew in a machine that took off and landed under full control. It was three years before another airplane succeeded—in 1906, Brazilian aviator Alberto Santos-Dumont made short flights in a motorized glider of his own design.

The next advances mainly involved materials. Steel and other alloys replaced wood for airframes, and aluminum panels instead of varnished cloth were used to cover them. Jets superseded gasoline engines, and just 44 years after the Wright brothers' first flight, an airplane flew faster than the speed of sound.

1913 U.S. biochemists discover Vitamin A.

1914 U.S. psychologist John Watson suggests that experiments with animals can be used to study human psychology.

1914 English military engineer Ernest Swinton proposes building the tank.

1913

1914

1913 Danish physicist Niels Bohr proposes a model of the atom in which negatively charged electrons orbit a positively charged neutron.

1914 English astronomer Arthur Eddington recognizes that nebulae are galaxies made up of millions of stars.

1914 The 40-mile (64 km) Panama Canal is completed between the Atlantic and Pacific Oceans.

Albert Einstein

Albert Einstein was the towering figure of science in the early 20th century. His ideas affected many areas of research and he updated the physics of Isaac Newton.

Albert Einstein was born in Ulm, in southern Germany, in 1879. His father was an electrical engineer, and Albert was extremely gifted in math and science at school. He found his German high school heavy handed, and in 1895, moved to Switzerland where he performed well. He then studied at a state higher educational polytechnic. Einsten took Swiss citizenship, and was offered a post in the Swiss patent office in 1902.

Albert Einstein teaching in 1921.

After teaching in Switzerland, Einstein returned to Germany in 1913. He remained in

TIMELINE
1914–1915

KEY:

- Biology and Medicine
- Engineering and Invention
- Astronomy and Math

1914 German engineer Oskar Barnack produces a prototype Leica camera.

1914 U.S. inventor Garrett Morgan produces a practical gas mask.

1915 U.S. astronomer Walter Adams identifies Sirius B as the first white dwarf star.

1915 U.S. surgeon Alexis Carrel performs open-heart surgery on a dog.

German soldiers on their way to war in 1914. Einstein turned his back on the extreme nationalism that other German academics displayed in 1914.

Germany throughout World War I. During the 1920s, his fame spread worldwide, and he was awarded many honors. In 1933, after Hitler came to power in Germany, Einstein moved to the United States and became a U.S. citizen. He died in the United States in 1955.

Timeline

1895 Einstein moves from Germany to study in Switzerland

1905 Publishes four influential papers: Brownian motion; the photoelectric effect; special relativity; the relationship of mass and energy

1915 Publishes his theory of general relativity

1921 Awarded the Nobel Prize in Physics

1933 Leaves Germany and renounces his citizenship

1939 Writes to U.S. President Roosevelt urging him to fund research into splitting the atom

1915 English inventor William Mills invents the Mills bomb, a type of hand grenade used during World War I.

1915 Several bacteriologists independently discover viruses that attack bacteria.

1915

1915 The German company Junkers makes the first all-metal, cantilever-wing airplane, the Junkers J-1.

1915 Scottish astronomer Robert Innes locates Proxima Centauri, the star nearest the sun.

Einstein (right) with Danish scientist Neils Bohr. Bohr was important in the development of quantum mechanics. Einstein had been involved in the creation of quantum mechanics, but later disagreed with the implications of the theory.

Einstein first came to international fame in the world of science in 1905. He not only wrote his PhD thesis (it was awarded in 1906), but also published four important papers. One was on Brownian motion, the seemingly random movement of small particles in a fluid. Einstein described the movement of pollen in a liquid and showed how it was related to the molecules of water.

A second paper looked at the so-called photoelectric effect, in which electromagnetic radiation such as light splits off electrons from a material that it strikes. Einstein described how light was not acting as a wave—the traditional way of describing a beam of light—but as a number of small packages of energy, which we now call photons. This insight that light could behave like a wave but

TIMELINE
1916–1917

KEY:

Biology and Medicine

Engineering and Invention

Astronomy and Math

Chemistry and Physics

1916 Several scientists make special alloys.

1916 French physicist Paul Langevin produces a primitive form of sonar.

1916

1916 German-born U.S. physicist Albert Einstein publishes his paper on the general theory of relativity, which mainly concerns gravity.

actually be composed of discrete units was vitally important for the development of quantum mechanics.

The third and fourth papers looked at a problem in the standard, classical theory of mechanics as outlined by Isaac Newton. This was to do with the behavior of an electromagnetic field. Einstein's work was particularly useful in terms of looking at behavior at high speeds, especially speeds approaching the speed of light and where there was no gravitational pull to consider. This theory was called special relativity on the basis that it mainly applied to such high speeds. The implications of special relativity were set out by Einstein in another paper, which described how mass and energy could be equivalent to each other.

Bending Rays of Light

Over the next few years, Einstein worked on his theory of special relativity, refining it to include gravity. He devised what is called his equivalence principle in 1907, and then, in 1911, estimated how the sun would bend a ray of light from outer space that passed close to its surface. In 1913, he published a paper together with mathematician Marcel Grossman, using a new type of geometry (now known as Riemannian geometry).

A cartoon of Einstein abandoning pacifism to involve himself in the fight against German oppression in the 1930s.

1917 The 100-inch (2.5 m) telescope is completed at Mount Wilson Observatory near Los Angeles.

1917 U.S. nurse Margaret Sanger opens the first birth control clinic in the United States.

1917

1917 The U.S. Black and Decker company markets the first electric hand drill.

1917 English engineer Archibald Low invents an electronic control system for rockets.

The first test of an atomic weapon, in New Mexico in 1945. Einstein had encouraged President Roosevelt to develop this weapon as early as 1939.

The final result was a new theory that he published in 1915, known as the general theory of relativity. This described how gravity worked, using a set of equations known as Einstein's field equations. Einstein described gravity as being linked to space and time—what he called spacetime, something that can be curved according to the energy and momentum of the matter and radiation present. The implication that time itself could be bent like a piece of string was shocking for many people, who ridiculed the idea. Even in the scientific community there were reservations about

TIMELINE
1918–1919

KEY:

Biology and Medicine

Engineering and Invention

Astronomy and Math

Chemistry and Physics

1918 German physical chemist Walther Nernst puts forward a theory of chemical chain reactions.

1918 U.S. company Kelvinator markets the first mechanical refrigerator for home use.

1918

1918 The world's most powerful radio transmitter begins operations at the naval station in New Brunswick, New Jersey.

Einstein's work, although he was awarded the Nobel Prize in Physics in 1921. However, in 1919, observations during an eclipse of the sun showed that Einstein's field equations and his theory of general relativity were correct. Then, in 1924, his paper on the photoelectric effect was confirmed after further work by Indian scientist Satyendra Bose, creating what are now called Bose-Einstein statistics.

The Atom Bomb

Einstein was a lifetime pacifist. He refused to join in the general German enthusiasm for the outbreak of war in 1914, and worked hard for international cooperation during the 1920s. After Adolf Hitler's rise to power in Germany he renounced his German citizenship, and helped German Jewish scientists to find posts worldwide. In 1939, he cosigned a letter with Hungarian-American physicist Leó Szilárd, urging President Roosevelt to fund research into splitting atoms. This letter, and personal representations Einstein made to Roosevelt, played a key part in obtaining support for the creation of the atom bomb.

The popular image of Einstein, as the brilliant scientist with wayward hair.

1918 U.S. chemist Winford Lewis develops the poison gas lewisite.

1918 U.S. embryologist Herbert Evans suggests that human body cells have 48 chromosomes each (in fact they have 46).

1919 U.S. astronomer Edwin Hubble begins his long study of Cepheid variable stars in the Andromeda Galaxy.

1919 Austrian zoologist Karl von Frisch describes the "dance" by which bees communicate with one another.

1919 English physicist Francis Aston develops the mass spectroscope for separating isotopes.

1918

1919

Synthetic Drugs

The mid- to late-19th century saw chemists declare war on pain. Some developments came from traditional cures, others came from experiments, and a few were luck.

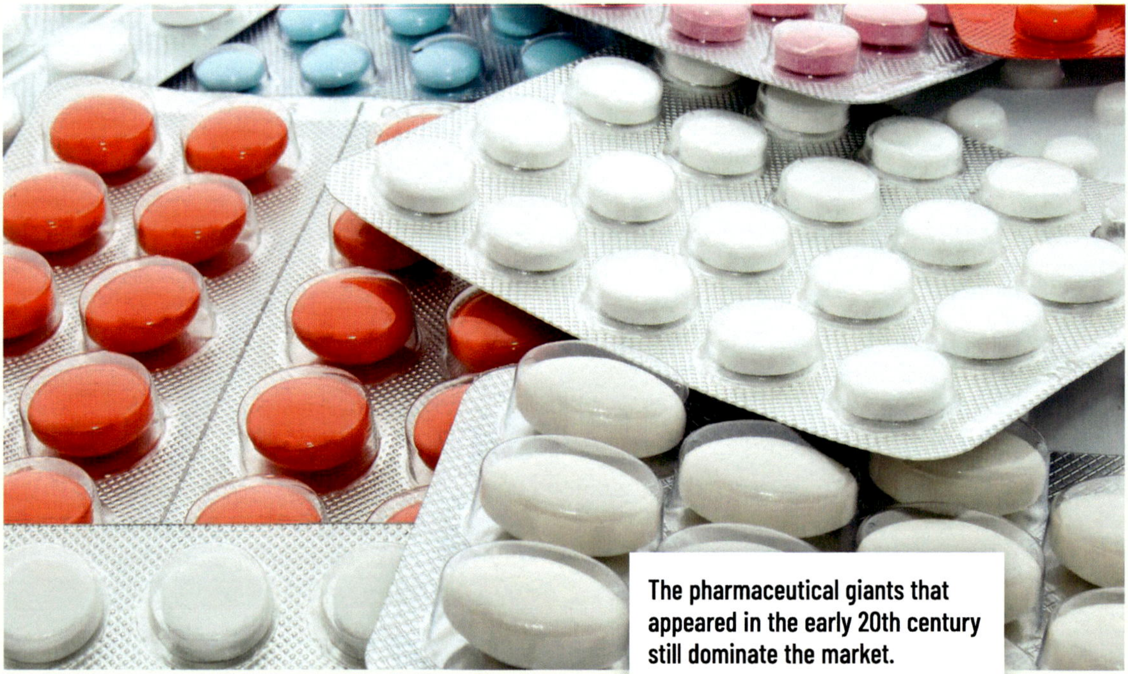

The pharmaceutical giants that appeared in the early 20th century still dominate the market.

TIMELINE
1919–1920

KEY:

Biology and Medicine

Engineering and Invention

Astronomy and Math

Chemistry and Physics

1919 New Zealand-born English physicist Ernest Rutherford reports that he has disintegrated nitrogen atoms by bombarding them with alpha particles.

1919

1919 British aviators John Alcock and Arthur Brown make the first nonstop flight across the Atlantic.

1919 U.S. psychologist John Watson suggests that behavioral conditioning should be a subject of psychological research.

Humans have used naturally occurring substances as medicines for thousands of years. Some of them, such as opiates, were used as analgesics (painkillers); but they were never very reliable, and they often had undesirable side effects.

First Synthetic Drugs

The first totally synthetic drugs were gases. In 1799, English chemist Humphry Davy discovered the painkilling properties of nitrous oxide, also known as laughing gas. In 1815, similar properties were noted for ether vapor. But amazingly, it was another 30 years before medical practitioners were to take advantage of their painkilling properties to perform surgery. In 1847, a stronger anesthetic gas, chloroform vapor, was developed by Scottish obstetrician James Simpson and used to help women during childbirth. None of the gases was free from side effects, notably that they made the patient unconscious, or at least insensible, and they were poisonous in large doses.

The use of certain plants to treat pain and fever has a long history. Ancient Egyptians used myrtle, ancient Greeks and medieval

Before modern drugs, people relied on traditional cures or treatments made up and sold by herbalists. Some cures contained naturally occurring drugs that may have had real benefits—but many were useless, and some were actually very harmful.

Timeline

1799 Laughing gas as painkiller

1815 Ether as painkiller

1828 Salicin isolated from willow

1847 Chloroform used in childbirth

1859 Salicylic acid in mass production

1899 Aspirin launched

1910 Salvarsan 606

1920 Scottish chemist Arthur Lapworth establishes the role played by electrons in organic chemical reactions.

1920 Ernest Rutherford predicts the existence of the neutron.

1920

1920 U.S. astronomer Vesto Slipher detects a redshift in light from galaxies, showing that they are receding (and that the universe is expanding).

1920 Station KDKA in Pittsburgh, Pennsylvania, begins the first regular radio broadcasts in the United States.

The Wonder Drug

Aspirin is by far the world's most popular synthetic drug. About 34 billion tablets are used every year in the United States. Aspirin forms the basis of many headache and cold cures; it is anti-inflammatory and reduces fever. It may also help reduce the risk of heart attacks and prevent some kinds of cancer.

Salicylic acid, extracted from willow, was once used to relieve fevers and pain. Aspirin consists of an ethanoyl (acetyl) derivative of salicylic acid.

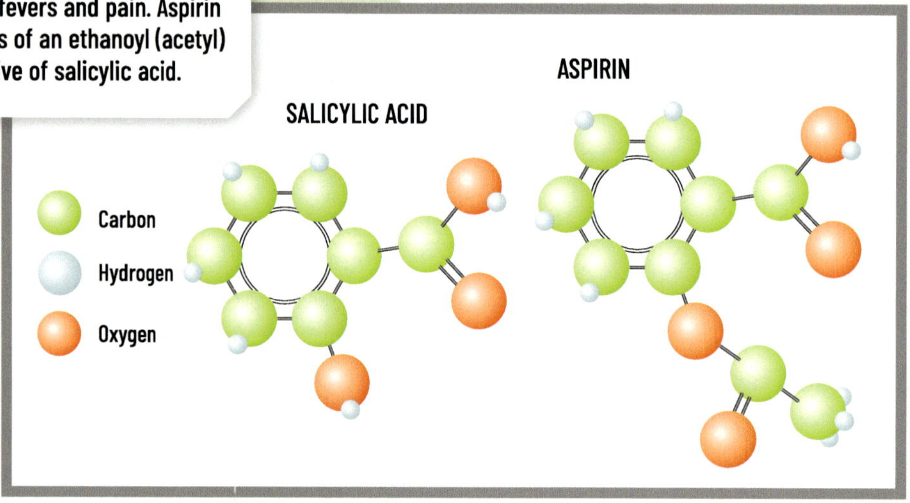

Europeans used willow and meadowsweet, and Native Americans used birch. All these plants contain the same active ingredient, called salicin after the scientific name for willow, *Salix*.

Wonderful Willow

The medicinal use of willow was rediscovered by English clergyman Edward Stone. In 1763, he reported that he had successfully used willow bark to reduce fever in 50 of his patients. The crucial breakthrough came in 1859, when a German chemist, Hermann

TIMELINE
1920–1922

KEY:
- Biology and Medicine
- Engineering and Invention
- Astronomy and Math
- Chemistry and Physics

1920 U.S. gunsmith John Thompson patents the Thompson submachine gun (Tommy gun).

1921 English economist John Maynard Keynes publishes his *Treatise on Probability.*

1921 U.S. airman John MacReady demonstrates spraying crops from an airplane.

Kolbe, figured out the chemical structure of salicylic acid and worked out how to synthesize it on a large scale—not from plants but from coal tar. The new drug went into mass production.

Willow is just one natural source of salicin; the chemical occurs in plants discovered and used independently by ancient peoples around the world.

Salicylic acid was an effective painkiller, but it caused stomachaches, so there was a need to modify the drug. The final steps were made by German chemist Felix Hoffman at the chemical company Bayer. He adapted French chemist Charles Gerhardt's earlier formula to synthesize acetylsalicylic acid, and in 1899 the new drug was launched by Bayer as aspirin. At first, only doctors could administer aspirin, but in 1915 it became available without prescription.

Another drug developed at about the same time as aspirin was phenacetin. It later led to the development of acetaminophen as a painkiller.

Modern Drugs

The therapeutic advancements of the 20th century meant the science of pharmaceutics had finally come of age. The ability to synthesize new compounds and tinker with their structure to modify their pharmacological effects is the basis of almost all modern drug development and is continually undergoing further adaptations.

1921 Canadian physiologist Frederick Banting isolates insulin, the hormone that controls glucose levels in the blood.

1922 German chemist Hermann Staudinger recognizes that substances such as rubber are natural polymers.

1921

1922

1921 The first expressway (Autobahn) opens in Germany.

1922 A Scottish team first uses insulin to treat patients with diabetes.

1922 The BBC (British Broadcasting Company, later Corporation) begins regular broadcasts in London.

Subatomic Particles

By 1920, physicists knew every atom consists of a nucleus carrying a positive electromagnetic charge surrounded by a cloud of electrons carrying a negative charge.

The paths of subatomic particles are traced through a cloud chamber.

TIMELINE

1923–1924

KEY:

- Biology and Medicine
- Engineering and Invention
- Astronomy and Math
- Chemistry and Physics

1923 Austrian doctor Sigmund Freud introduces his theory of the subconscious mind.

1923 Scottish engineer John Logie Baird invents a television system that uses mechanical scanning.

1923

1923 U.S. physical chemist Gilbert Lewis defines an acid as a substance that accepts electrons.

1923 U.S. physicians George and Gladys Dick isolate the bacteria that cause scarlet fever.

Ernest Rutherford, the New Zealand-born English physicist, found that when he bombarded nitrogen atoms with alpha particles (helium nuclei), hydrogen nuclei were released. In 1920, Rutherford suggested the name "proton" (from the Greek *protos,* meaning "first") for the hydrogen nucleus.

Smashing Particles

Rutherford's research continued to center on smashing atomic nuclei by bombarding them with alpha particles. In 1925, English physicist Patrick Blackett, working under him, developed the cloud chamber into a device for recording the disintegration of atoms. But alpha particles were not powerful enough to smash large nuclei, which repelled them without disintegrating. More energetic impacts were needed, and in 1932, English physicist John Cockcroft and Irish physicist Ernest Walton built the world's first particle accelerator at the Cavendish Laboratory. It used powerful electromagnets to accelerate protons that were then directed at a target.

Timeline

1920 Proton named

1925 Cloud chamber invented in 1911 developed further

1932 First antimatter particle, positron, discovered; neutron identified

1934 Neutrino identified and named

1937 Muon discovered

Ernest Rutherford oversaw much of the early research into subatomic particles. However, the major breakthrough relied on the development of particle accelerators that were able to create more powerful collisions between particles.

1923 Austro-Hungarian rocket scientist Hermann Oberth introduces the idea of escape velocity, the speed needed to leave Earth's gravity.

1924 English watchmaker John Harwood patents a self-winding wristwatch.

1924 Swedish chemist Theodor Svedberg builds the ultracentrifuge.

1923

1924

1923 The German Benz company makes the first trucks with diesel engines.

1924 A team of U.S. pilots make the first round-the-world flight (they stop only to refuel).

1924 The Computing-Tabulating-Recording Company changes its name to International Business Machines (IBM).

Scientists check part of the Large Hadron Collider, which shoots particles around a 17-mile (27 km) underground loop in Switzerland.

Nature of Radiation

In 1932, French physicists Irène and Frédéric Joliot-Curie found that alpha bombardment of paraffins or similar hydrocarbons (compounds of hydrogen and carbon) led to the emission of protons with very high energy. English physicist James Chadwick, working at the Cavendish Laboratory, conducted experiments that suggested that this high-energy radiation consisted of particles with approximately the same mass as the proton, but carrying no electromagnetic charge.

Chadwick thought the new particle was a proton bound to an electron (a hydrogen atom), and he was able to calculate the mass of the particle. Because it carries no charge, unlike electrons, the particle came to be called the "neutron."

In 1930, Wolfgang Pauli—one of the greatest physicists of the 20th century—was studying beta radiation, a stream of electrons emitted by unstable atoms. The electrons seemed to lose energy, but no explanation could be found for the loss. Pauli's solution was to propose that beta radiation also contains a previously unknown particle with the unusual properties of possessing no

TIMELINE

1925–1926

KEY:

- Biology and Medicine
- Engineering and Invention
- Astronomy and Math
- Chemistry and Physics

1925 English physicist Patrick Blackett begins experiments with colliding atoms in a cloud chamber.

1925 U.S. pathologist George Whipple discovers iron in red blood cells.

1925

1925 U.S. astronomer Edwin Hubble introduces a classification scheme for galaxies.

1925 Black American biologist Ernest Just shows that UV radiation can cause cancer.

charge and no mass when it is at rest. The particle was later named the "neutrino."

During the late 1920s, theoretical physicists were very interested in the properties of electrons. American physicist Carl Anderson discovered the particle later called "positron" in 1932, as did Patrick Blackett in 1933. It was the first antimatter particle to be identified.

Building the Atom Splitter

In 1932, John Cockcroft and Ernest Walton charged a hollow metal chamber to 400,000 volts and injected protons into it. The positively charged particles were driven away from the high positive voltage along a series of tubes kept at lower voltages. They struck a piece of lithium. Alpha particles (helium nuclei) that were formed in the interaction caused flashes on an observation screen and were then photographed.

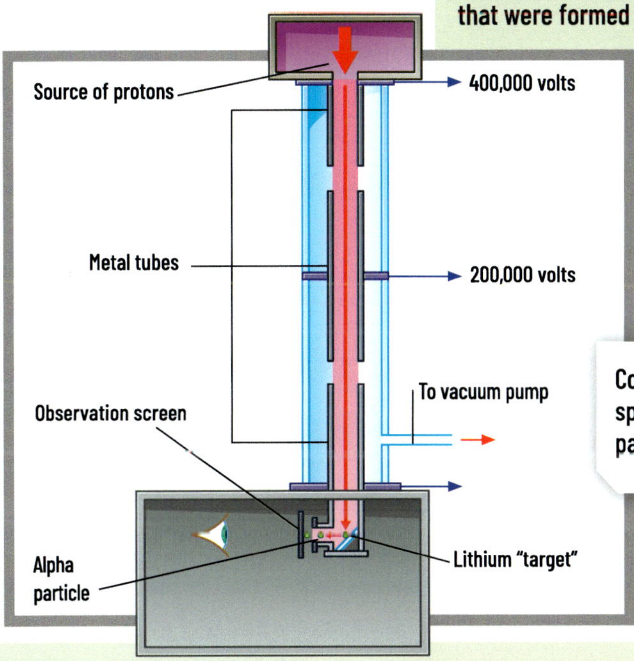

Cockcroft and Walton's atom splitter was the world's first particle accelerator.

1926 U.S. physical chemist Gilbert Lewis coins the word photon to describe a quantum, or particle, of light.

1926 Norwegian inventor Erik Rotheim invents the aerosol can.

1926

1926 U.S. geneticist Hermann Muller produces genetic mutations in fruit flies by exposing them to radiation.

1926 U.S. inventor Robert Goddard successfully launches a liquid-fuel rocket.

The First Television

In October 1925, Scottish electrical engineer John Logie Baird transmitted the first television pictures in his London workshop.

John Logie Baird produced this early portable television in 1949.

TIMELINE
1927–1928

KEY:

- Biology and Medicine
- Engineering and Invention
- Astronomy and Math
- Chemistry and Physics

1927 English zoologist Charles Elton publishes *Animal Ecology*, establishing the science of ecology.

1927 German theoretical physicist Werner Heisenberg formulates his uncertainty principle.

1927

1927 English chemist Nevil Sidgwick introduces the modern theory of chemical valence, the role of electrons in chemical bonds.

1927 U.S. aviator Charles Lindbergh makes the first solo flight across the Atlantic Ocean.

John Logie Baird was born in the west of Scotland and educated in Glasgow. His poor health cost him his job as an electrical engineer, and after three failed businesses he retired to live in the southern English coastal town of Hastings in 1922. It was there that he began experimenting with television.

Timeline

1923 Zworykin invents iconoscope TV camera tube

1925 Baird's first television pictures

1929 BBC begins experimental TV broadcasts

1937 BBC begins commercial TV broadcasts

1938 Zworykin receives patent for iconoscope TV camera tube

1941 CBS begins experimental color TV broadcasts

Capturing an Image

All television cameras require some way of scanning an image. Baird used a rapidly spinning Nipkow disk patented by Polish electrical engineer Paul Nipkow in 1884. It is a disk—Baird's was made from cardboard—pierced with a spiral of holes. As the disk rotates, an observer looking through it sees an object as a series of curved lines or scans, each of which is produced by a different hole in the disk. The first pictures of 1925 were of a ventriloquist's doll named Stooky Bill. The first live subject (in 1926) was an office boy who worked in premises below Baird's London workshop. At first, Baird sent his television images along wires. By 1927, pictures were sent along a telephone line, and a year later he sent pictures over the Atlantic telegraph cable to New York.

Baird poses with his early apparatus, including a Nipkow disk with a spiral of holes that scan an image as a series of lines as the disk rotates.

1928 U.S. astronomer Henry Russell determines that hydrogen is the most abundant element in the sun's atmosphere.

1928 U.S. mathematician John von Neumann outlines the foundations of game theory.

1928

1928 English theoretical physicist Paul Dirac predicts the existence of antimatter particles.

1928 Scottish bacteriologist Alexander Fleming discovers the antibiotic penicillin.

First TV Camera

The iconoscope was developed by Vladimir Zworykin in 1923 (patented 1938). An electron beam from an electron gun scans an image focused onto a photosensitive plate. Deflection plates make the electron beam scan in lines from side to side. Light striking the plate gives it a positive charge. Electrons not held by the charge bounce to another electrode and form the video signal.

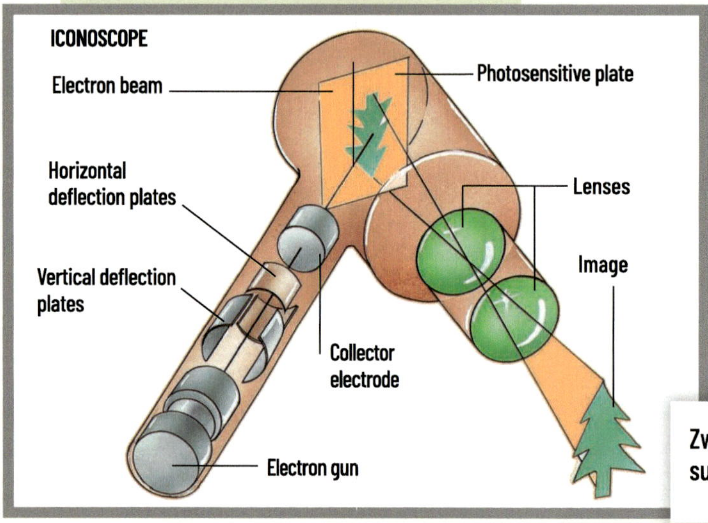

Zworykin's iconoscope was the first successful television camera tube.

In September 1929, the British Broadcasting Corporation (BBC) began experimental television broadcasts using Baird's mechanical system. The flickering images consisted of only 30 lines, later increased to 60 and eventually 240 lines. In 1932, Baird transmitted pictures by shortwave radio. The experimental broadcasts ended in 1935. By the time commercial television broadcasting started in Britain in 1937, the BBC had adopted the 405-line electronic system developed by the British company Marconi-EMI.

World War II halted television broadcasting. Before the end of the war, Baird had produced color television and three-dimensional images as well as a widescreen system (by projection) and stereophonic sound. He could not complete this work as he died before television broadcasting had

TIMELINE
1928–1929

KEY:
- Biology and Medicine
- Engineering and Invention
- Astronomy and Math
- Chemistry and Physics

1928 U.S. aviator Amelia Earhart is the first woman to fly across the Atlantic.

1928 U.S. inventor Jacob Schick patents the electric razor.

1929 German biochemist Adolf Butenandt successfully isolates the female sex hormone estrogen.

1929 German-born U.S. physicist Albert Einstein announces his unified field theory, which attempts to bring all the fundamental forces into a single theory.

1928 1929

resumed. When it finally started again, it used an all-electronic system.

Electronic Systems

Scottish engineer Alan Campbell-Swinton figured out the principles of an electronic system in 1908, although at that time the apparatus was not available to put his ideas into practice. In the United States, Russian-born Vladimir Zworykin went down the electronic route from the start with his iconoscope. U.S. inventor Philo Farnsworth developed a similar camera in 1927. Zworykin joined RCA and soon improved his system. In 1941, CBS made experimental color broadcasts from station WCBW in New York, although regular transmissions in color did not begin until 1951.

Cathode Ray Tube

The cathode ray tube, invented in 1897 by German physicist Ferdinand Braun, is the heart of a television receiver. Like the iconoscope, it has an electron gun and deflection plates and a coil to focus the electron beam onto the screen at the front. A phosphor, which gives off light when struck by electrons, coats the inside of the screen on which the scanned image builds up line by line.

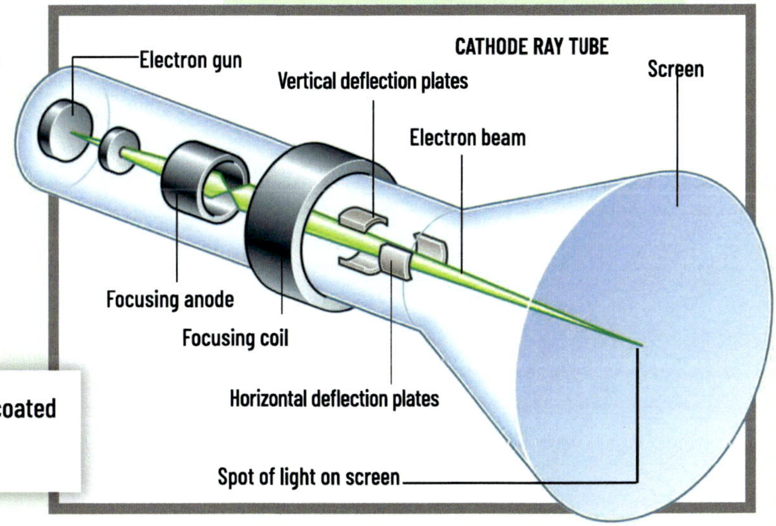

The screen of the cathode ray tube is coated with chemicals called phosphors.

1929 German engineer Felix Wankel patents his rotary engine.

1929 Japanese geophysicist Motonori Matuyama suggests that Earth's magnetic field has undergone reversals several times in its history.

1929

1929 A German Zeppelin airship makes a 21-day around -the-world flight.

1929 U.S. astronomer Edwin Hubble formulates a law that relates the distance of a star to the speed with which it moves away from Earth.

Penicillin and Antibiotics

In the early part of the 20th century, millions of people died each year from bacterial infections. But the discovery of a mold that could kill germs would change all that.

The *Penicillium* mold grows in moist, nutrient-rich substances.

TIMELINE
1930–1931

KEY:

Biology and Medicine

Engineering and Invention

Astronomy and Math

Chemistry and Physics

1930 English engineer Frank Whittle invents the gas turbine (jet) engine.

1930 U.S. businessman Clarence Birdseye markets the first quick-frozen foods.

1930

1930 U.S. astronomer Clyde Tombaugh discovers the planet Pluto (now classed as a dwarf planet).

1930 U.S. engineer Vannevar Bush builds an analog computer.

From the late 19th century, thanks to the work of French chemist Louis Pasteur and others, scientists and medical practitioners recognized a new type of enemy—bacteria, or "germs." Many bacteria had been identified, and the conditions they caused in humans were better understood.

Discovery of Penicillin

Wound infection was the specialized area of Scottish bacteriologist Alexander Fleming. Unlike other medical researchers of the time, Fleming believed that the way to tackle infection was to harness natural processes to destroy infection through biological cures.

In 1928, after returning from vacation to his laboratory in London, Fleming noticed something unusual about a culture of *Staphylococcus* bacteria that he had left developing in a petri dish. In his absence, a mold had grown in the dish, and it appeared to be killing the *Staphylococcus*. Fleming identified the strange mold as a species of

Timeline

1877 Pasteur observes anthrax-killing bacteria

1921 Fleming discovers lysozyme in living cells

1928 Fleming identifies penicillin

1940 Mice and humans treated with penicillin

c.1943 Penicillin in mass production

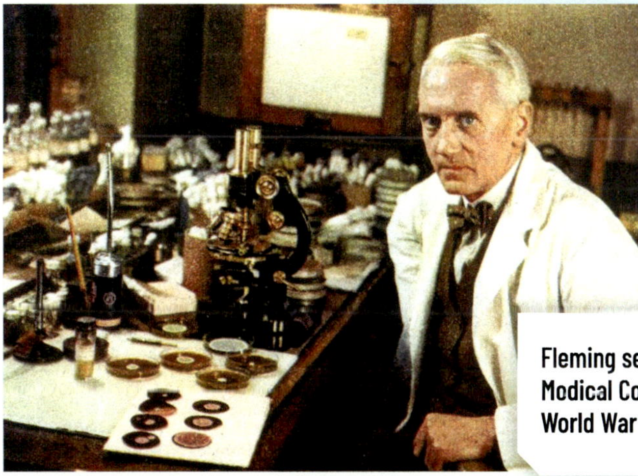

Fleming served in the Medical Corps during World War I.

1930 Austrian-born Swiss physicist Wolfgang Pauli predicts the existence of the neutrino.

1930 U.S. chemist Wallace Carothers discovers neoprene, leading to the production of nylon.

1931 U.S. pathologist Ernest Goodpasture devises a way of growing viruses in chicken eggs.

1931 U.S. chemist Linus Pauling explains the nature of benzene.

1931 U.S. radio engineer Karl Jansky accidentally discovers radio waves from space, leading to the science of radio astronomy.

1930

1931

What's in a Name?

"Antibiotic" means "destroyer of life." Antibiotics destroy the bacteria causing illness. In 1877, Louis Pasteur noticed that anthrax cultures died when mixed with other bacteria. In 1889, Frenchman Paul Vuillemin named the process by which one organism kills another "antibiosis." From that came the word "antibiotic," first used by U.S. biochemist Selman Waksman in 1941. He received a Nobel Prize in 1952 for his discovery of Streptomycin, the first successful treatment for tuberculosis.

Penicillium and discovered that the liquid it produced (penicillin) was just as effective at destroying a large number of different bacteria. More exciting still, it appeared to have no effect on healthy living tissue, so Fleming thought it could be safe to use on humans. But there were drawbacks. For a start, there were several disease-causing bacteria—notably those responsible for plague and cholera—on which it had no effect at all. Even more disheartening was the fact that penicillin turned out to be difficult to produce.

Manufacturing Penicillin

The problems seemed insurmountable at first, but in 1939, a group of scientists at Oxford University in England began following up Fleming's discovery. The team was led by Australian pathologist Howard Florey and German biochemist Ernst Chain. By 1940, they extracted penicillin and began testing it on mice.

Fleming in his laboratory. His work was followed up by an international team of scientists.

TIMELINE
1932-1933

KEY:

Biology and Medicine

Engineering and Invention

Astronomy and Math

Chemistry and Physics

1932 Synthetic rubber is first marketed in the United States under the name Duprene.

1932 U.S. physicist Ernest Lawrence operates the first cyclotron, one of the first particle accelerators.

1932

1932 British and Irish physicists carry out the first nuclear fission.

1932 The Sydney Harbor Bridge is completed in Australia.

Penicillin enabled mice to fight off infections that otherwise would have killed them. Thanks to refinements in the production technique developed by English biochemist Norman Heatley, the "miracle" drug was being mass-produced in the United States and Britain by about 1943.

The development could not have come at a more crucial time. World War II was raging, and wounded servicemen were the first to benefit. Thousands of lives were saved, at least on the Allied Forces' side. After the war, the benefits of penicillin were spread more widely. Fleming, Florey, and Chain received the 1945 Nobel Prize in Medicine. Heatley was recognized by an honorary degree from Oxford University in 1990.

Penicillin saved the lives of many wounded soldiers treated at field hospitals during World War II.

1933 The Tasmanian wolf becomes extinct in the wild.

1933 English aviator Alan Cobham devises a system for refueling airplanes in flight.

1933 Swiss astrophysicist Fritz Zwicky suggests that space must contain invisible "dark matter" (to explain the total mass of the universe).

1933 English engineer Alan Blumlein patents a system of stereophonic sound recording.

1933

1933 Polish and English chemists synthesize vitamin C, the first vitamin to be artificially produced.

1933 The Boeing 247, the first modern airliner, goes into commercial service.

The Development of Radar

During the 1920s and 1930s, researchers realized that radio reflection could provide a way of detecting planes and other objects such as ships and icebergs.

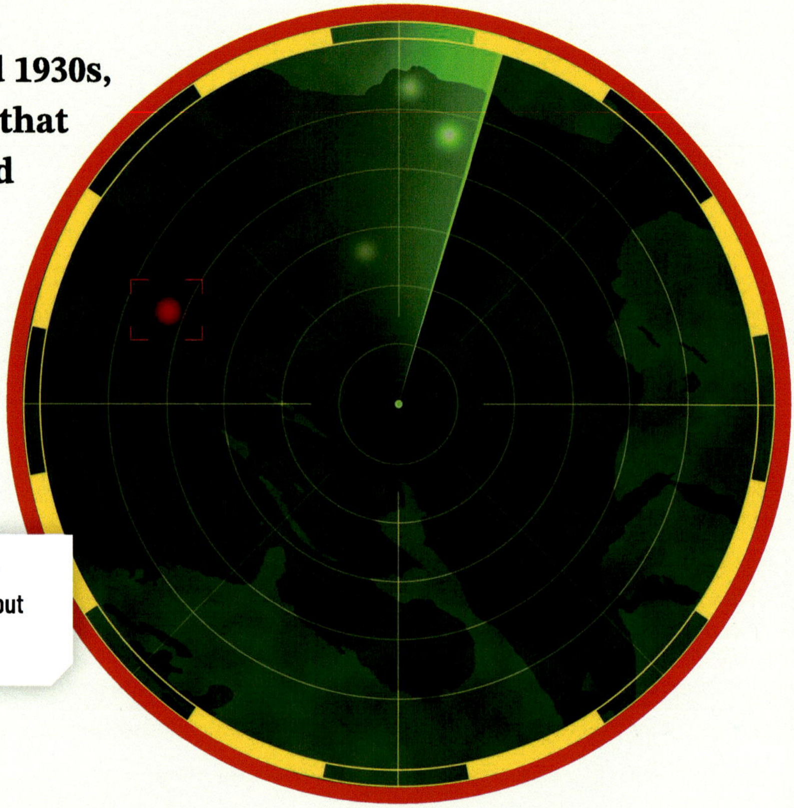

Radar screens are familiar from many war movies about submarines or ships.

TIMELINE
1934–1935

KEY:

- Biology and Medicine
- Engineering and Invention
- Astronomy and Math
- Chemistry and Physics

1934 Astrophysicists studying supernovas predict the existence of neutron stars.

1934 U.S. scientist Royal Raymond Rife tests a cancer-curing treatment using radio waves.

1934

1934 Dutch physicist Hendrik Casimir explains the phenomenon of superconductivity.

1934 U.S. psychologist B. F. Skinner invents the Skinner box for studying the psychology of animals.

Radar stands for "radio detecting and ranging," which explains exactly what the process does. To detect a plane, a radar set transmits a pulse of very high-frequency radio waves (microwaves), and a receiving antenna picks up any radio echoes that return. The direction of the returning signal reveals the direction of any target present, and its range can be calculated from the time it takes for the microwave signal to travel out and back.

Timeline

1904 Christian Hülsmeyer's patented radar

1921 Magnetron

1922 U.S. Naval Research Laboratory experiments

1935 Robert Watson-Watt's patented radar

1938 Klystron

1938 Radar set installed on USS *New York*

1940 Cavity magnetron

First Steps

In 1904, German engineer Christian Hülsmeyer took out the first patents for such a device. His system used continuous waves (not radio pulses) to warn ships of possible obstructions. In 1922, engineers at the U.S. Naval Research Laboratory in Washington, D.C., sent radio signals across the Potomac River and detected passing ships when they interrupted the radio beam. In Britain, the Scottish physicist Robert Watson-

In 1904, Christian Hülsmeyer patented a primitive radar system to warn ships of obstructions.

1934 English inventor Percy Shaw patents "cats eyes," reflecting road markers.

1935 U.S. seismologist devises the Richter scale to measure earthquake intensity.

1935 U.S. physicist Arthur Dempster discovers the isotope uranium-235. It is later used in atom bombs.

1935

1934 In France, Citroën launches the first mass-produced, front-wheel-drive car.

1935 U.S. amateur photographers invent Kodachrome transparency film.

1935 Portuguese neurologist António Egas Moniz introduces prefrontal lobotomy as a treatment for some personality disorders.

The Cavity Magnetron

A cavity magnetron is at the heart of microwave devices, including radar. A filament inside a block of conductive material (the anode block) generates electrons. These are concentrated into a cloud by a magnetic field. As the cloud passes vanes inside the anode block, the electric charges generate a vibrating electromagnetic field. An antenna picks up the vibrations, which travel out through a waveguide as microwaves.

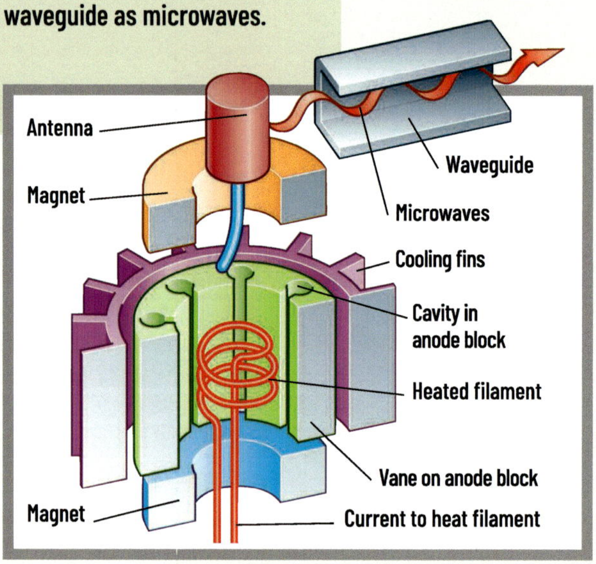

Watt was asked to investigate the possibility of using radio beams as "death rays" to attack enemy pilots. Using a BBC transmitter, he detected a Heyford bomber flying 7 miles (11 km) away at a height of 9,800 feet (3,000 m). By September 1938, with World War II approaching, the British built a chain of radar antennas on towers 330-feet (100 m) high along the eastern and southern coastlines of England. They were able to detect incoming airplanes at a range of up to 200 miles (320 km).

Engineers also adapted radars to aim guns, particularly antiaircraft guns and (in Germany) long-range naval guns. In the United States, a radar system was installed on the battleship USS *New York* in February 1938.

TIMELINE

1936–1937

KEY:

Biology and Medicine

Engineering and Invention

1936 U.S. chemist Robert Williams announces the structure of vitamin B1.

1936 The British Supermarine Spitfire fighter airplane makes its maiden flight.

1936

1936 The first giant panda is captured alive in the wild.

Later Advances

Modern radar antennas sometimes resemble golf balls. This one guides aircraft toward an airport runway.

The very high frequencies of radar signals require special electronics. Early transmitters used a vacuum tube called a magnetron. An improved version came in about 1934 from the French company CSF, invented by Henri Gutton. Two researchers at Birmingham University, John Randall and Henry Boot, developed a new device in 1940. It generated wavelengths as small as 3.5 inches (9 cm), and a radar using it could detect a submarine periscope 7 miles (11 km) away. The British government immediately gave details of this "cavity magnetron" to researchers in the United States.

After World War II, radar found a wide range of peacetime applications, such as air traffic control and ship navigation. In 1946, astronomers picked up radar signals reflected back from the moon, and in 1958 echoes came back from the planet Venus. NASA has used probes to map the bottom of Earth's oceans and the surface of Venus. Weather forecasters use satellite radar, as do many law enforcement agencies to catch speeding motorists.

1937 U.S. electrical engineer George Stibitz makes a binary adding machine.

1937 The Golden Gate Bridge is completed in San Francisco.

1937 The Swiss company Nestlé begins selling instant coffee (Nescafé).

1937

1937 U.S. physicist Chester Carlson invents xerography, a dry photocopying process.

1937 Swiss-born Italian pharmacologist Daniel Bovet identifies the first antihistamine substance that is effective in treating allergies.

Wernher von Braun

Wernher von Braun was a German-trained engineer and pioneer rocket scientist who became an American citizen and worked on NASA's successful space program.

The V-2 rocket represented the pinnacle of von Braun's wartime achievements.

TIMELINE
1938–1939

KEY:

- Biology and Medicine
- Engineering and Invention
- Astronomy and Math
- Chemistry and Physics

1938 The asteroid Hermes approaches closer to Earth than any previous observed asteroid: 485,000 miles (780,000 km).

1938 German physicists induce nuclear fission in uranium.

1938

1938 U.S. chemist Roy Plunkett synthesizes the "nonstick" plastic PTFE (Teflon).

1938 South African professor J. L. B. Smith identifies a coelacanth, a fish previously thought to be extinct.

As a boy, Wernher von Braun read science fiction books by Jules Verne and H. G. Wells. He went on to study engineering at Berlin and Zurich universities. From 1930, he made experimental rockets for the German Society for Space Travel. Rocket testing was banned in Germany under the terms of the Versailles Treaty (signed in 1918 after World War I), so he worked on ballistics. The ballistics and munitions branch of the German army, led by rocket engineer Walter Dornberger, noticed his activities. With the backing of Adolf Hitler, von Braun went to the newly established rocket research center at Peenemünde on the Baltic Sea coast where, in 1936, he became its director.

Timeline

1936 Von Braun director of Peenemünde rocket center

1942 Launch of first A-4 (later V-2) rocket

1946 Von Braun works at White Sands in the United States.

1958 *Explorer I*, the first U.S. satellite

1962 Glenn's orbital flight in *Mercury* capsule

1969 The *Apollo* moon landing

Vengeance Weapon

At Peenemünde, von Braun's greatest achievement was the "vengeance weapon" 2 (V-2). Originally designed by Dornberger in 1941 as the A-4, the huge rocket used liquid oxygen and alcohol as fuel, weighed over 11 tons, and delivered a warhead containing 1.1 tons of explosives. Its launch speed of 2,500 feet (760 m) per second carried it high into the upper atmosphere, then it came down

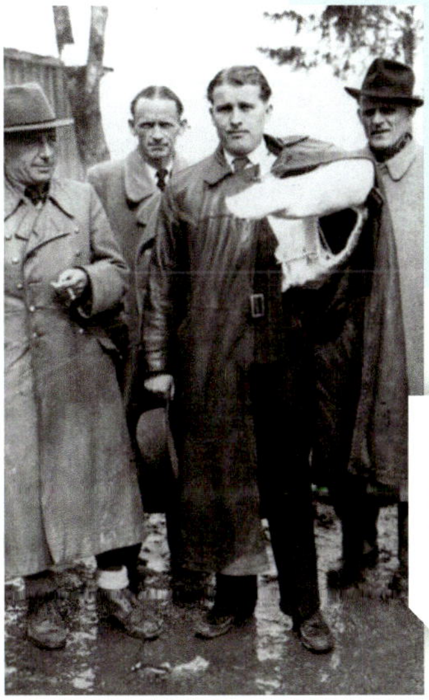

Wernher von Braun (his arm in a cast) surrenders to the Americans in 1945.

1938 German engineer Ferdinand Porsche designs the Volkswagen "Beetle" car.

1939 U.S. physicist John Atanasoff makes a prototype electronic binary calculator.

1938

1939

1938 Hungarian-born Argentine inventor Laslo Biró makes a prototype of the first ballpoint pen.

1939 French chemist Marguerite Perey discovers the radioactive element francium.

An American soldier examines a partly built V-2 rocket at the end of World War II.

The V-2 Rocket

The V-2 was the forerunner of all modern rockets. Von Braun based its development on papers written early in the 20th century by the U.S. rocket pioneer Robert Goddard. Its engine was designed to fire for up to 65 seconds, to bring the rocket to the upper reaches of the atmosphere. At that stage, the engine cut out and the rocket angled itself to begin to fall toward its target.

silently toward a target 200 miles (320 km) away at over three times the speed of sound. Many of the V-2s launched from 1944 fell on Antwerp in Belgium, and in London.

At the end of World War II, von Braun chose to surrender to the U.S. Army and went to the United States. From 1946, he worked at White Sands Proving Ground, New Mexico, and in

Londoners clear wreckage left by one of nearly 1,400 V-2 raids on the British capital.

TIMELINE
1939–1940

KEY:
- Biology and Medicine
- Engineering and Invention
- Chemistry and Physics

1939 Physicist Albert Einstein tells President F. D. Roosevelt that nuclear chain reactions would lead to the building of bombs.

1939 Swiss chemist Paul Müller realizes the insect-killing properties of DDT.

1939

1939 The National Broadcasting Company (NBC) begins regular TV transmissions in the United States.

1939 U.S. zoologist Victor Shelford introduces the concept of biomes (major geographical areas that support their own range of organisms).

1950 moved to the Ballistic Missile Agency at Huntsville, Alabama. There he adapted a V-2 to carry a nuclear warhead, creating the Redstone missile. Von Braun became an American citizen in 1955 and was recruited by the National Aeronautics and Space Administration (NASA). In 1958, he oversaw the successful launch of *Explorer I*, the United States's first artificial satellite. He headed the team that built the *Mercury* capsules for the U.S. crewed spaceflight program. In 1960, he became director of the Marshall Space Flight Center, developing the giant three-stage *Saturn V* rocket for NASA's Apollo missions. The climax came in 1969, when American astronauts landed on the moon. Von Braun retired from NASA in 1972. He died on June 16, 1977.

Controversial Figure

At the end of World War II, Wernher von Braun and his team surrendered to the U.S. Army. Von Braun later said he wanted to make sure that knowledge of the weapon he had created would pass into the right hands. He and his team of technicians were secretly relocated to the United States. Their past records of working for Nazi Germany were covered up. The U.S. authorities believed that rocket technology was more valuable than punishing the scientists for their role in the war.

The rockets displayed at the Kennedy Space Center in Florida are all based on Von Braun's basic designs.

1940 Three heavy radioactive elements are identified, including plutonium, by U.S. physical chemist Glenn Seaborg.

1940 The Tacoma Narrows suspension bridge in Washington State collapses because of oscillation.

1940

1940 British and Australian scientists extract and purify penicillin and perform the first clinical trials of the drug.

1940 U.S. zoologist Donald Griffin announces that bats "echolocate" using ultrasound.

Nuclear Fission

In the early 20th century, physicists realized that bombarding atoms with subatomic particles could release huge amounts of energy in a process called nuclear fission.

The best-known use of nuclear fission was in the creation of the atom bomb.

TIMELINE
1941–1942

KEY:

Biology and Medicine

Engineering and Invention

Astronomy and Math

Chemistry and Physics

1941 German computer pioneer Konrad Zuse completes his third computer (the Z3).

1941 English chemists produce the plastic Dacron (Terylene), later licensed to U.S. company DuPont.

1941

1941 Soviet nuclear physicists observe spontaneous nuclear fission in uranium.

1941 U.S. biochemist Selman Waksman coins the term "antibiotic" to describe new bacteria-killing drugs.

Danish scientist Niels Bohr explained the principles behind nuclear fission.

In 1932, John Cockcroft and Ernest Walton experimented with high-energy protons in the particle accelerator at the Cavendish Laboratory in Cambridge, England. In Paris in 1934, Irène and Frédéric Joliot-Curie found that proton bombardment sometimes produced radioactive isotopes. Two years later, Enrico Fermi found neutrons were more effective than protons when used to smash atoms.

Splitting the Atom

In 1939, Otto Hahn and Fritz Strassmann identified the products of uranium bombardment. Hahn and Strassmann had demonstrated that the uranium nuclei had broken apart. "Fission" had occurred. The same year, Lise Meitner and her nephew Otto Frisch, working with Niels Bohr, explained this result.

Timeline

1932 Cockcroft and Walton particle accelerator

1934 Joliot-Curies produce radioactive isotopes

1936 Fermi uses neutrons to smash atoms

1939 Hahn and Strassmann identify products of uranium fission

1942 First nuclear reactor

1945 First atom bomb tested

1951 Nuclear reactor built to generate electricity

Italian physicist Enrico Fermi designed the first working nuclear reactor. It was operational at Chicago University in 1942.

1942 French diver Jacques Cousteau invents the aqualung, or scuba.

1942 Italian-American physicist Enrico Fermi achieves the first controlled nuclear chain reaction, at the University of Chicago.

1942

1942 U.S. radio astronomer Grote Reber compiles the first radio map of the universe.

1942 German rocket engineer Wernher von Braun makes the V-1 and V-2 flying bombs.

1942 The Manhattan Project, to make an atom bomb, begins in the United States.

Uranium Fission

Fission occurs when an atomic nucleus breaks in two with the release of two or three neutrons. It can be induced by firing neutrons or protons at a nucleus. Fission releases an amount of energy equal to the energy that bound the nucleus together. When a neutron strikes a ^{235}U atom, the nucleus absorbs it, becoming ^{236}U, which divides into two lighter nuclei with the release of neutrons. If the neutrons strike other ^{235}U nuclei, they too undergo fission, setting up a chain reaction.

Hahn and Strassmann found that as well as a large amount of energy, uranium fission released neutrons that may trigger fission in uranium nuclei, which then create the possibility of a chain reaction.

The Power of Fission

At the start of World War II, Bohr and John Wheeler published a paper describing the complete fission process. Meanwhile, Francis Perrin showed a certain "critical mass" of uranium is needed to sustain a chain

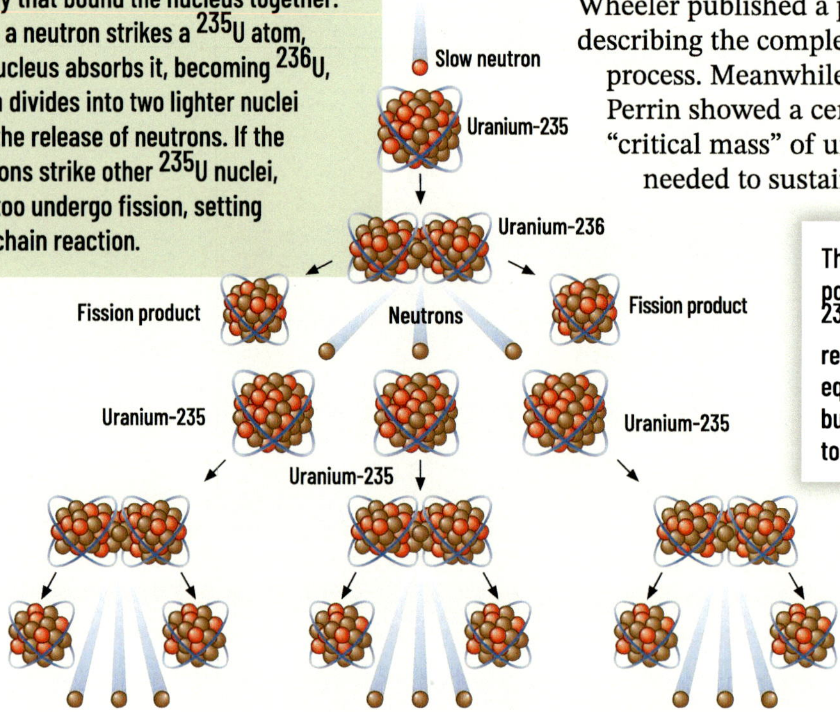

The fission of 2.2 pounds (1 kg) of ^{235}U nuclei releases energy equivalent to burning 3.3 million tons of coal.

TIMELINE
1943-1944

KEY:

Biology and Medicine

Engineering and Invention

Astronomy and Math

Chemistry and Physics

1943 U.S. scientists build the world's first operational nuclear reactor at Oak Ridge, Tennessee.

1943 Japanese physicist Sin-Itiro Tomonaga describes the basic physical principles of quantum electrodynamics.

1943

1943 English mathematician Alan Turing oversees the building of Colossus, an electronic stored-program computer.

1943 Dutch-born U.S. physician Willem Kolff builds the first kidney dialysis machine.

Scientists watch a controlled chain reaction in the "atomic pile" at the University of Chicago in 1942. Because of the radiation, no photographs could be taken, so the event was recorded by an artist.

reaction. Designed by Fermi, the first working reactor began operating in 1942, at the University of Chicago. In 1951, the Experimental Breeder Reactor in Idaho became the first reactor to generate electricity.

It became clear that a sustained fission reaction could be used to create a bomb of immense power. Work to develop an atom bomb began in Britain and the United States. The two programs merged in August 1942 to form the Manhattan Project. The first successful test took place in New Mexico on July 16, 1945. Atomic bombs were dropped on the Japanese cities of Hiroshima and Nagasaki in August 1945.

1943 U.S. company Dow Corning is set up to make silicone plastics.

1944 U.S. workers at IBM complete the Harvard Mark I calculator.

1943

1944

1944 U.S. physical chemist Glenn Seaborg isolates the radioactive elements americium and curium.

Undersea Exploration

One of the great achievements of 20th century science was to enable humans to explore the seabeds of the world's deep oceans.

It is often said that we know more about the surface of the moon than we do about the surface of the seabed. Technology has only allowed people to explore the ocean depths from the mid-20th century. It took sustained efforts by scientists and explorers, and developments in medical understanding of the dangers of going into the depths, to make such exploration possible.

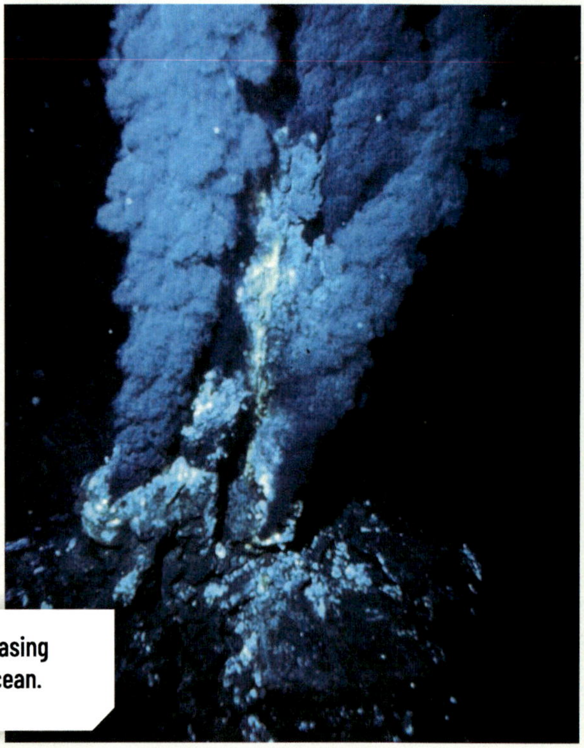

A hydrothermal vent releasing hot gas in the Atlantic Ocean.

Deep-Sea Dangers

The most obvious barrier to undersea exploration was that humans need oxygen to breathe. Before the invention of diving suits and other aids, they could not stay underwater for long periods of time. Another obstacle was that water pressure increases with depth. This has serious effects on the way the

TIMELINE

1944–1945

KEY:

Biology and Medicine

Engineering and Invention

Chemistry and Physics

1944 Russian-born U.S. engineer Igor Sikorsky builds the VS-36A, which sets the design of the modern helicopter.

1944 U.S. physicist Robert Dicke makes a radiometer for detecting microwave radiation.

1944

1944 U.S. chemist Robert Woodward leads the synthesis of the antimalarial drug quinine.

1944 U.S. bacteriologist Oswald Avery shows that nearly all organisms have DNA as their hereditary material.

A replica of the diving machine that John Lethbridge invented in 1715.

Timeline

1715 John Lethbridge invents a diving machine

1878 Paul Bert works out that "the bends" is caused by bubbles in the bloodstream

1943 Jacques-Yves Cousteau uses a prototype scuba apparatus for the first time

1960 *Trieste* descends to 35,814 ft (10,916 m) below the ocean surface in the Mariana Trench

2018–2019 *Limiting Factor* submarine dives to the lowest points of the Atlantic, Southern, Indian, Pacific, and Arctic Oceans

human body reacts. Temperature also causes complications for undersea exploration. The greater the depth from the surface, the colder it becomes.

Diving suits and machines were first invented in the 18th century. In 1715, John Lethbridge built a "diving machine." This looked like a wooden barrel and had metal straps around it to help it resist water pressure. The diver lay flat on his stomach and looked out through a round window. The two armholes had oiled

1945 U.S. government scientists make and test an atom bomb.

1945 Soviet physicist Vladimir Veksler designs and builds a powerful particle accelerator, the synchrocyclotron.

1945

1945 English crystallographer Dorothy Hodgkin uses X-ray crystallography to determine the structure of penicillin.

1945 Chinese-American biochemist Choh Hao Li isolates the human growth hormone somatotropin.

Paul Bert realized that decompression was the cause of "the bends."

leather seals to prevent water from entering the barrel. Air was pumped into the machine before it was sealed and lowered into the water on ropes. By the 1830s, the modern diving suit had been invented. This was a waterproof suit and a large helmet with a glass face mask. Air was pumped into the suit through a tube attached to a boat at the surface. Calculating the exact composition of the air in the tubes was difficult. It varied according to the depths at which the divers were working. Water pressure affects the way the body is able to absorb gases.

The Bends

Early diving suits were cumbersome, but they enabled divers to stay underwater for long periods. However, it was soon discovered that as divers tried to go down deeper, they often became sick when they came back up to the surface. The sickness was known as "the bends," because these divers suffered from severe bone and joint pains that caused them to double over. The bends is caused by gases, principally nitrogen, that are dissolved in the bloodstream, forming bubbles as the diver surfaces to a less pressured environment. French physiologist Paul Bert was the first person to realize that this sickness was caused by decompression. The solution was to allow time in a decompression chamber so that the diver would gradually become accustomed to a different kind of pressure.

TIMELINE
1946–1948

KEY:

Biology and Medicine

Engineering and Invention

Astronomy and Math

Chemistry and Physics

1946 U.S. computer engineers build ENIAC (Electronic Numerical Integrator and Computer), a fully electronic computer.

1946 U.S. engineer Percy Spencer invents the microwave oven.

1946

1946 U.S. chemist Willard Libby begins work on radiocarbon dating, a chemical way to date old organic material.

1946 English engineer Frederic Williams makes a computer memory using a cathode ray tube.

Scuba Apparatus

Early diving suits did not allow for much freedom of movement. The breakthrough in this came during the 1940s and 1950s, with the development of scuba gear. Scuba stands for self-contained underwater breathing apparatus. A self-contained breathing apparatus had been invented in 1926, but allowed for only a short duration underwater. In 1942, French engineer Émile Gagnan invented a demand regulator that made air use more efficient. This was further developed by French oceanographer Jacques-Yves Cousteau over the next two decades. From the 1990s onward, the gas used in the tanks has been nitrox, which contains more oxygen than atmospheric air.

Deep Diving

Scuba diving equipment enabled divers to explore many undersea habitats. However, scuba diving has its limits. Most scuba dives take place in water no more than 130 feet (40 m) deep. The deepest scuba divers ever go is 2,000 feet (610 m). They wear "atmospheric suits," designed to protect them against water pressure, and breathe specific mixtures of gas in their tanks.

A scuba diver exploring a coral reef.

1947 Italian biologist Rita Levi-Montalcini finds nerve growth factor (NGF) in chick embryos.

1947 U.S. architect Buckminster Fuller invents geodesic dome construction for large buildings.

1948 U.S. physicists propose a big bang theory for the origin of the universe.

1947

1948

1947 U.S. airman Charles "Chuck" Yeager makes the first supersonic flight, in a Bell X-1 rocket-propelled airplane.

1947 U.S. inventor Edwin Land demonstrates the Polaroid camera.

1948 U.S. musician Leo Fender and his colleagues market the first solid-body electric guitar.

Trieste, the bathyscaphe used by the U.S. Navy to explore the Mariana Trench in the Pacific.

Submersibles

In the 1920s, bathyspheres were built to explore the great depths of the oceans. A bathysphere descended to 3,028 feet (923 m) in 1930. An even stronger underwater craft, the bathyscaphe, was developed in the 1940s. It could adjust its own buoyancy and reach extreme depths. In 1960, Jacques Piccard and Lieutenant Donald Walsh descended 35,814 feet (10,916 m) into the Challenger Deep, the deepest part of the seabed in the Pacific Ocean's Mariana Trench, in the bathyscaphe *Trieste.*

These submersibles had to be extremely strong to resist the water pressure at such depths, and vision through the small windows of thick, toughened glass was limited. They did, however, show scientists sights such as thermal vents on the ocean floor, where the unique conditions create life in an environment unlike any on Earth's land surface.

TIMELINE
1948–1949

KEY:

- Biology and Medicine
- Engineering and Invention
- Astronomy and Math
- Chemistry and Physics

1948 U.S. brothers Harold and Horace Babcock detect the sun's magnetic field.

1948 U.S. biochemists introduce the use of cortisone to treat rheumatoid arthritis.

1948

1948 U.S. physicists Richard Feynman and Julian Schwinger independently formulate new versions of quantum electrodynamics.

1948 U.S. electrical engineer Peter Goldmark invents the long-playing phonograph record.

Robot Explorers

The dangers of undersea exploration were tragically illustrated by the loss of the submersible carrying passengers to view the wreck of the ocean liner *Titanic* in 2023, which was lying on the seabed of the North Atlantic Ocean. The challenges of building craft that can operate in the deepest seas mean that the next stage of underwater exploration will probably rely on remotely piloted craft and robots. In 1985, robot submarines had been used to locate the wreck of *Titanic* before a craft was built to take people down to it. Much of the current knowledge of the deep ocean bed does not come from visual recording, but from the results of sonar (sound navigation and ranging) sweeps that give scientists the general topography of the ocean floor. Sound travels farther in water than radar or light waves.

Limiting Factor is a deep-sea exploration craft that has made crewed dives in all five oceans of the world.

1949 U.S. microbiologists culture the virus that causes poliomyelitis.

1949 U.S. chemists produce the radioactive element berkelium by bombarding americium with alpha particles.

1949 U.S. astronomer Frank Whipple suggest that comets are "dirty snowballs," consisting mainly of ice and rocky debris.

1949

1949 The first jet airliner, the de Havilland Comet, flies in England.

1949 English chemists use pulses of light in flash photolysis, for analyzing ultrafast chemical reactions.

1949 U.S. computer pioneers John Eckert and John Mauchly construct BINAC, a binary automatic computer.

Glossary

amplifier An electronic device that increases the strength of an input current or voltage.

antibiotic A chemical substance that can destroy or inhibit the growth of bacteria or other microorganisms.

atom The smallest unit into which matter can be divided and still retain its chemical identity.

bacillus A cylindrical-shaped bacterium.

bacteria (singular bacterium) Microscopic organisms that can cause disease.

cathode The negative electrode of a battery or similar device, through which an electric current passes.

cathode ray A stream of electrons emitted by a cathode when heated.

electron A negatively charged subatomic particle.

enzyme A large protein molecule that acts as a catalyst for the chemical reactions on which life depends.

neutron An uncharged subatomic particle in the atomic nucleus.

nuclear reactor A device for generating electricity by nuclear fission or nuclear fusion.

nucleus, atomic (plural nuclei) The positively charged dense region at the center of an atom, composed of protons and neutrons.

photon The basic particle of energy in which light and other forms of electromagnetic radiation are emitted.

proton A positively charged subatomic particle in the atomic nucleus.

radar An acronym for radio direction and ranging; a device that uses radio waves for detecting distant objects.

radioactivity The emission of particles or radiation by atomic nuclei.

subatomic particle Any particle that is smaller than an atom.

vaccine A preparation containing viruses or other microorganisms introduced (often by injection) into the body to stimulate the formation of antibodies and build up immunity against infectious disease.

virus A tiny parasitic organism that can only reproduce inside the cell of its host.

Further Information

Books

Avery, Bryan Patrick. *Black Men in Science.* Rockridge Press, 2022.

Bayarri, Jordi. *Albert Einstein and the Theory of Relativity* (Graphic Science Biographies). Lerner Publishing Group, 2020.

Gunderman, Dr Richard. *Marie Curie* (Pioneers of Science). Rosen Publishing, 2022.

Isaacson, Walter. *Albert Einstein.* Rosen Publishing, 2022.

Pellum, Kimberley Brown. *Black Women in Science.* Rockridge Press, 2019.

Trusty, Kathy. *Black Inventors: 15 Inventions That Changed the World.* Rockridge Press, 2021.

Washington, Danni. *Bold Women in Science.* Rockridge Press, 2021.

Winter, Ali and Mickael El Fathi. *Science and Me. Inspired by the Discoveries of Nobel Prize Laureates in Physics, Chemistry, And Medicine.* Lerner Publishing Group, 2021.

Websites

interestingengineering.com/lists/7-of-albert-einsteins-inventions-that-changed-the-world
Seven of Einstein's most significant theories that changed the world.

www.atomicarchive.com/science/fission/index.html
Simple guide to the basics of nuclear fission from the Atomic Archive, with diagrams, videos, and links.

www.encyclopedia.com/people/science-and-technology/space-exploration-biographies/wernher-von-braun
Pages from Encyclopedia.com on Wernher von Braun and his importance to the development of rockets and the space age.

www.nobelprize.org/alfred-nobel/biographical-information/
The Nobel Prize official site, with a biography of Alfred Nobel, and links to all the prize winners and other useful information.

Publisher's note to educators and parents: Our editors have carefully reviewed these websites to ensure that they are suitable for students. Many websites change frequently, however, and we cannot guarantee that a site's future contents will continue to meet our high standards of quality and educational value. Be advised that students should be closely supervised whenever they access the internet.

Index